Evocations
of
Four Quartets

Evocations
of
Four Quartets

paintings by David Finn

BLACK SWAN BOOKS

*The publisher expresses thanks to both Faber and Faber (London)
and Harcourt Brace Jovanovich, Publishers (U.S.A.)
for permission to reproduce excerpts from
works by T. S. Eliot.*

This book was published on the occasion of an exhibition
at the Yale Center for British Art, New Haven,
Connecticut, September 22–November 18, 1990.

Publication of this book was assisted by a grant
from George and Virginia Ablah of New York.

Published by
Black Swan Books Ltd.
P. O. Box 327
Redding Ridge, CT 06876
U.S.A.
ISBN 0-933806-61-2 (cloth)
ISBN 0-933806-62-0 (paper)   *Printed in Japan.*

CONTENTS

Preface

One can see why T. S. Eliot was strongly opposed to the idea of his poems being illustrated. Besides being rich in visual images, there are whole passages in his poetry which are word-pictures suggesting paintings of scenes drawn from life or nature. *The Waste Land* contains many lines which seem almost to ask for illustration, e.g. "These fragments have I shored against my ruins" or—as caricature—Mr. Eugenides, "The Smyrna merchant / Unshaven, with a pocket full of currants / C.i.f. London." Sometimes the reader feels the influence of impressionistic, Whistlerian paintings in the London scenes: "The river sweats / Oil and tar / The barges drift / With the turning tide / Red sails / Wide / To leeward, swing on the heavy spar."

The objection to illustrating such word-pictures with paintings—rendering them back into a medium from which they sometimes seem to derive—is that to do so would be to make the verbally impressionistic become pictorially literal. It would be to lock a door of the poet's imagination which should be left open. One can understand Eliot objecting to this.

What is true of *The Waste Land* is even more true of *Four Quartets* in which the verbal imagery evokes nature, the seasons, different in each section. First, there is the England of summer and old houses and gardens in "Burnt Norton," then in the "Dry Salvages" there is the Mississippi of the poet's childhood in the American South. Later on there are the coast of Massachusetts, London during the Blitz, etc. Any of these might inspire the illustrator, using Eliot's text as clues or pointers. But all such attempts would have the effect of leading the mysteriously evocative poetry into dead-ends of the too literally seen.

There are, however, ways in which the visual artist's image may be illuminating. One such—paradoxical as this may seem—can happen when Eliot is at his most abstract. We use in common parlance the phrase "the line of argument." An argument does have a line and sometimes to visualize it can be helpful. To me one of the most revealing of David Finn's paintings (1) is that in which there is one red and one mauve sinuous line pointing towards a spot of pure yellow, on the page opposite the opening lines of "Burnt Norton":

> Time past and time future
> What might have been and what has been
> Point to one end, which is always present.

This painting visualizes the line of thought here, which in the poetry is not imagistic—unless perhaps there is a suggestion of the visual in the phrase "point to one end": but the reader, I think, dismisses this because to "see it" in the poetry would be to see the phrase as a cliché. Here David Finn, in visualizing the abstract language, happily illuminates Eliot's "line of argument" without intruding on it.

In his introduction, David Finn explains that these paintings record images which occurred to him as the result of his obsessive immersion in the poetry over a number of years. He got to know the whole of *Four Quartets* by heart. Here is the transformation of the poet's sensibility into terms of the painter's. It is a process of submission and there is a deep humility about it.

Sometimes the work draws attention to a gap between the poet's visual sensibility and that of the artist, especially when a passage of Eliot's suggests to Finn an object literally seen, while at other times lines of Eliot provoke in the painter's mind visions parallel to the poetry. One of the most successful examples of this (2) is the shape like a lump of torn-up earth with roots dangling from it and a whirling halo of leaf or flower or insect marks above—the painter's response to the passage about faces seen in the limbo of the London Underground in "Burnt Norton."

An ambiguous area of experience in *Four Quartets*, as in much of Eliot's poetry, is a dark sensuality. This is ground where the painter might well feel that angels do not dare to tread. But it is just here that David Finn perhaps comes nearest to being literal without betraying Eliot. The painting (10) that faces the "Adam's curse" passage of "East Coker" is very striking and very true.

In some of these paintings the artist helps the reader to understand the poetic process itself—the continuity and extension of the vision—behind the writing, its visual structure. This happens in the painting (2) that accompanies the passage beginning "Here is a place of disaffection." The painting visualizes Eliot's "slow rotation suggesting permanence." He follows the development of the visual procedure through "rotating," "whirling," "eructation," being "driven on the wind," in the poetry. He forcefully realizes the visual hint contained in the phrase with which the passage culminates, about the "twittering world," in the small jabbing marks contained within a bushy pattern which suggests, perhaps, the invasion of a tree on Hampstead Heath (a phenomenon I have witnessed) by starlings. The implication of such an event (the hint of it) is implicit in the poetry—injected into the reader's mind—and taken up—without being interpreted literally by the painter.

This artist succeeds best, I think, when he is visualizing the temporal historic or metaphysical progression of argument and imagery which underlies the ever-forward movement of the poet, on his spiritual journey through the worlds of time and eternity, in *Four Quartets*. Sometimes contrasts of darkness and light are realized in scenes and objects and figures projected. Sometimes though, they are near-abstractions—contrasted planes of darkness or light with differing surfaces. Often when the painter is being less literal or figurative than Eliot is being in the corresponding passage in the poetry, he helps us understand the poetry better than when he comes near to depicting the poetry with images of figures suggested to him by it.

In the third section of "East Coker" there is the passage:

And we know that the hills and the trees, the distant panorama
And the bold imposing facade are all being rolled away—
Which shall be the darkness of God. As, in a theatre,
The lights are extinguished, for the scene to be changed
With a hollow rumble of wings, with a movement of darkness on
  darkness.

Here Mr. Finn avoids the obvious temptation to give us something of the theatre, and takes up only "a movement of darkness on darkness." There are two thin, broken white lines drawn horizontally across an oblong panel of deep electric blue, almost black (9). The painting (8) preceding this is of vertical flame-spirals on an almost black screen through which spots of vermilion show, and with edges like torn paper, invoking the famous passage beginning: "O dark dark dark. They all go into the dark."

One of the recurring themes of *Four Quartets* is of history as a pattern of interweaving movements in time. This motif culminates in a dazzling painting (37), like an evocation of the sea, far out, and consisting of waving white and blue broken lines, leading to the horizon and sky.

I began by writing that Eliot objected to the idea that his poems should be "illustrated." But very few of the paintings can, to my mind, be considered as illustration. Only very occasionally does the painter launch out into pure picturalization of some scene or some figure which Eliot's poetry has suggested to him. These are, I think, the least successful. The justification of others, of the successes—and there are many of these—is that they are not illustrations but obsessions. They help the reader not by making him think "the poetry *looks* like this," but by setting up a kind of apposition—projecting a pictorial form which throws light on the poetry without imitating it, and which the poetry conversely throws light on. The best of these paintings—especially in some of the more abstract ones—throw light on the continuity of the thought in certain passages of *Four Quartets.*

In his introduction, David Finn most movingly bears witness to his passion for the poetry—his total absorption in it for several years. This increases one's awed admiration for the poet and also for this wholly dedicated reader. After looking at these paintings I realized things about the *Four Quartets* which I had not realized before: above all, the sense of its being a journey through time and eternity.

Stephen Spender

Introduction

In 1943 when *Four Quartets* was first published as an entirety, I was working as a salesman on the night shift of a bookshop in New York City. During the day, I had a full program of courses at The College of the City of New York where English was my major. Eliot was at best a shadowy figure for me at the time, since James Joyce was the dominant literary personality in my life, and *Finnegans Wake* the masterpiece I hoped one day to master. Of almost equal importance was Sir James G. Frazer's *The Golden Bough* and I can still remember the joy of acquiring all twelve volumes of the complete edition and reading through them, notes and all. I knew about Joyce's involvement with the folklore and mythology of the world, but I was not aware that Eliot had an equally profound sense of the truths contained in those mysterious metaphors of human experience.

I was then full of expectation and anticipation about life, but a number of my friends were cynical and bitter about the state of the world, and it was they who considered Eliot's *The Waste Land* something of a cult poem. I remember them quoting its famous lines almost incessantly as if everything wrong with the way things were, was perfectly described in its unforgettable phrases. The spiritual element in Eliot's thinking evident in *Ash Wednesday* was far less interesting to them. And when *Four Quartets* arrived, it was not greeted (as far as I knew) with any great excitement. At the bookstore, we did sell a few copies of the new poem, but it seemed to make little or no impression on my generation. Its mood seemed to be radically different from what had first made Eliot famous, and no one I knew thought it contained that quality of greatness which had been considered the mark of his genius.

About twenty years later I saw a slim volume devoted to a commentary on *Four Quartets* on the coffee table of a poet friend of mine, Lenore Marshall. I briefly thumbed through it and found it so interesting that I later bought a copy for myself. Reading that book proved to be the beginning of an experience which had a profound influence on my life. The poem which had then meant so little to me in my twenties became an obsession in my forties and fifties.

As I read and re-read the poem from the first passage where the word "perhaps" heralds the existential uncertainties which appear throughout ("Time present and time past / Are both perhaps present in time future") until the majestic symbolism of the closing line which declares that "the fire and the rose are one"—virtually every word carried resounding overtones that reverberated throughout my being. It is a poem of strange and provocative paradoxes which hint at truths beyond our comprehension: "The still point of the turning world . . . in my beginning is my end . . . what you are is what you are not . . . what you do not know is the only thing you know . . . the way up is the way down . . . the end is where we start from." Implicit in these enigmatic phrases are virtually indescribable, inexpressible essences of reality. They seemed to me to be magic incantations, and along with many other passages, they drew me with increasing intensity into the haunting rhythm of the poem and its mystical, overwhelmingly compelling statements about human experience.

I took to carrying a paperback copy of the book in my pocket so that I could repeat passages from it on subway and taxi rides or while waiting to meet people in offices or at lunch. After a while my copy became so worn that I had to buy a new one, and then another . . . and another. Today I have sixteen worn copies of the poem which are a record of my determination to plumb the depths of this profound work.

After months of unending fascination, I decided that the only way I could possibly absorb the full meaning of the poem would be to memorize all 876 lines, and over a period of time I managed to accomplish what was for me quite a feat. Then the words really became my own. I possessed them as I had never possessed a poem before, and I could repeat the lines over and over to myself in an effort to discover what lay behind them. I also read every commentary I could find on the poem, including books by Helen Gardner, Hugh Kenner, F. O. Matthiessen, Elizabeth Drew, Allen Tate,

Frank Kermode, Stephen Spender, Robert Sencourt, George Williamson. I especially appreciated a series of articles written on the poem by my friend James Johnson Sweeney. What turned out to be one of the most valuable sources was a phrase-by-phrase exploration of the poem by Peter Milward, *A Commentary on T. S. Eliot's "Four Quartets"* (published in 1968 by The Hokuseido Press in Tokyo).

But in the end, the most telling interpretation of the poem to me was in my own head, and I felt I had to find a way to get it out onto a surface where I could react to it visually. It was then that I decided to begin a series of paintings which would try to portray my inner feelings about each passage. This proved to be a deeply emotional exploration (which I later repeated with Yeats' "Byzantium" poems as published in the Black Swan Books edition of that series).

What I found so satisfying about the act of creating these paintings was the development of a graphic idea that would enable me to explore what the words pointed to but could never fully explain on their own ("Words," wrote Eliot, "strain, / crack . . . slip, slide, perish, / Decay with imprecision . . ."). Many of the visual representations were extremely personal. Others were conceptual. All sought to express what I discovered about myself and the world around me as I digested and re-digested the passages. My purpose was not to paint what was on the *writer's* mind but what the words brought out in *my* mind, and the series became a sort of spiritual autobiography. It represented what came into my head through a probing study of what seems to me to be the most evocative poem I have ever encountered.

When working on the paintings inspired by the first quartet, "Burnt Norton," I had the uncanny feeling that the poem was coming alive inside me. "Time past and time future . . . point to one end which is always present" (1) seemed to contain the essence of a great truth—or perhaps *the* great truth—about existence. In an almost mystical way, which I tried to echo in red and blue lines curving around a yellow circle, these few words expressed what Alfred North Whitehead described as "actual concretions," the elementary events which contain everything that happened in the past, everything that is happening now, and everything that is potential in the future. The wonderful phrase "All is always now"—perhaps my favorite line in the whole poem—miraculously positioned the mind to witness the reality of eternity. It inspired me to paint a picture (3) of a precious Chinese vase (suggested by "Chinese jar" of the passage) which was the first present I bought the eighteen-year-old girl who later became my wife. Broken and mended many times over the years, it still remains filled with memories and love.

The feeling of personal identification became even stronger in the second quartet, "East Coker." The painting for the opening lines "In my beginning is my end" (4) seemed to be my very sense of self evoked in line and color. "Out at sea the dawn wind / Wrinkles and slides" (5) reminded me of the months that I was stationed on the coast of Florida during World War II, watching the ocean in its many transformations. The passage beginning with the words "O dark dark dark. They all go into the dark" gave me the opportunity to make a statement about the appetite for recognition which is not one of our most commendable traits, yet seems to play such a central role in our lives. The lines "I said to my soul, be still, and let the dark come upon you" inspired a black-on-black painting with subtle nuances and delicate white lines, revealing in the darkness the way to inner peace and personal salvation. A painting of two lovers standing together and apart represented the first man and woman and all those who followed (including my wife and me), facing the consequences of "Adam's curse," surrounded by "purgatorial fires," and knowing that "to be restored, our sickness must grow worse" (10).

When painting "the middle way" (11), a friend of mine committed suicide in the middle of his way, and I was so disturbed that for a period of weeks my eyesight was badly distorted. I suffered from double vision, which I recorded in the painting as a way of commemorating that searing experience. The "old stones that cannot be deciphered" (12) were stones I had picked up in my travels and which I thought were filled with especially mysterious meanings—one from a beach of black stones near Lyme Regis on the southern coast of England which my wife and I had found strangely moving; the second from the excavation at Jericho which brought me into proximity with my ancient Biblical heritage; the third from the ground around the Parthenon which I have long considered one of the places in the world which all should see before they die—if they can (I once arranged to send a young friend of mine who had terminal cancer to see the Parthenon as a way of expressing my great affection for him); and the fourth which I picked up on the Island of Iona, which Kenneth Clark described as one of those rare sites where one can feel a profound sense of mystery and spirituality in the ground beneath one's feet.

By the time I reached the third quartet, "Dry Salvages," I felt that this series of paintings was becoming the story of my life. I liked the idea that "Old men ought to be explorers" (13) because I didn't believe in the concept of retirement from one's work, and I was determined that as I became older, I would find fulfillment in the continuing search for new horizons. For "The agony of others nearly experienced / Involving ourselves" (15) I used as my subject a relief self-portrait by Käthe Kollwitz—which hangs on my study wall—she sculpted after her friend Ernst Barlach died. "Time the destroyer is time the preserver" (16) is a painting of the line which both divides and unifies our lives.

In the fourth quartet, "Little Gidding," I began with a scene from the Catskill Mountains which had been a second home for me in my childhood and where I became especially aware that "Midwinter spring is its own season" (17). Two paintings (19 and 20) depict a branch of a beautiful dogwood tree outside our bedroom window—first, "with transitory blossom of snow," as I watched it many times in winter; second, as it appeared "white again, in May with voluptuary sweetness."

Sometimes I found the words of a particular passage so ingeniously fitted together that they became themselves the image in my painting. That's how I felt about the lines "And what you thought you came for / Is only a husk of meaning / From which the purpose breaks only when it is fulfilled" (21). For the stanzas which had to do with "The death of air," "The death of earth," and "The death of water and fire," I depicted the elements of nature with different colors representing their varied aspects (22, 23 and 24).

I have never been able to read Dante in Italian and have had to be satisfied with English translations. I was especially excited, therefore, by the Dantesque section of "Little Gidding" which I felt might have the same grandeur as *The Divine Comedy* in its original language. My painting of "Some dead master" was intended to be an embodiment of both Dante's Virgil and Eliot's Dante (25). In the succeeding paintings from this section, I alternated between abstractions, as in "So I assumed a double part" (26), and figurative representations, as in ". . . the cold friction of expiring sense" (28), depending on whether the meaning was intended to be symbolic or sensate.

A wonderful crab apple tree, which our family calls "the marrying tree" because all of our four children were married under it, seemed to be an ideal choice for the lines "All shall be well, and / All manner of thing shall be well" (32). The veins of a blazing red autumn leaf struck me as a surreal but apt way to represent the lines "The dove descending breaks the air / With flame of incandescent terror" (34). "Every poem an epitaph" (36) was another one of those rare lines which I thought deserved to be its own image. And for ". . . the source of the longest river" (38), I tried to combine the most delicate colors with a river curving along the spiral of life, indicating that in the end the poet had discovered the ultimate truth of being.

When I had finished the paintings, it struck me that there was an inner meaning in *Four Quartets* which could be discovered in its structure. I became aware that each of the four sections had a major theme accompanied by carefully constructed variations. "Burnt Norton's" theme is the enchainment of time and the discovery of the still point. "East Coker's" theme is death, not as an end but as a beginning. "Dry Salvages" presents the ocean-like rhythm of the flow of life, and the way to freedom. "Little Gidding" portrays the futility of history, and man's ultimate redemption through spiritual knowledge. In the five movements of each section, the same basic pattern can be identified. And not only is the pattern of the poetry in each section similar, but the relation of that movement to each section's basic theme is likewise. Studying this overall scheme helped me to grasp the monumentality of Eliot's vision and the vastness of a creation that I thought came close to comprehending the essential mystery of life and death.

When plans were being made to exhibit and publish this series of paintings, together with the relevant quotations from the poem, I mentioned the project to the editor at Faber and Faber who was responsible for Eliot publications. I knew that Eliot did not like the idea of having his poems "illustrated" and I wanted to make sure that my "evocations" were consistent with his wishes. The editor advised me that Mrs. Valerie Eliot could not agree to anything that would lead readers to think that the Eliot Estate has sanctioned my paintings as "illustrations" of the text. In this regard, she had referred to a letter written by her husband to his friend Djuna Barnes in 1949 in which he stated, "Personally the idea of an illustrated edition is as antipathetic to me as illustrated editions of my poems have always been." I explained that I had no intention to create illustrations for the poem but that my purpose had been to create visual counterparts to the multitude of meanings I found in certain lines of the poem, and that my paintings were intended to stand on their own. The editor agreed that these were quite different from illustrations, and that it would be appropriate for me to proceed with the project.

Eliot once wrote that if he is to be remembered by posterity, it will be for *Four Quartets.* Whether or not time will prove him correct is yet to be known, but I hope my series of paintings will offer some testimony to its profound and lasting effect on one reader for whom its evocative passages charted an unforgettable voyage of self-discovery.

David Finn

Evocations
of
Four Quartets

1

Time past and time future . . .
Point to one end, which is always present.

2

Here is a place of disaffection . . .

3

. . . all is always now.

4

In my beginning is my end.

5

Out at sea the dawn wind
Wrinkles and slides.

6

Had they deceived us
Or deceived themselves. The quiet voiced elders . . . ?

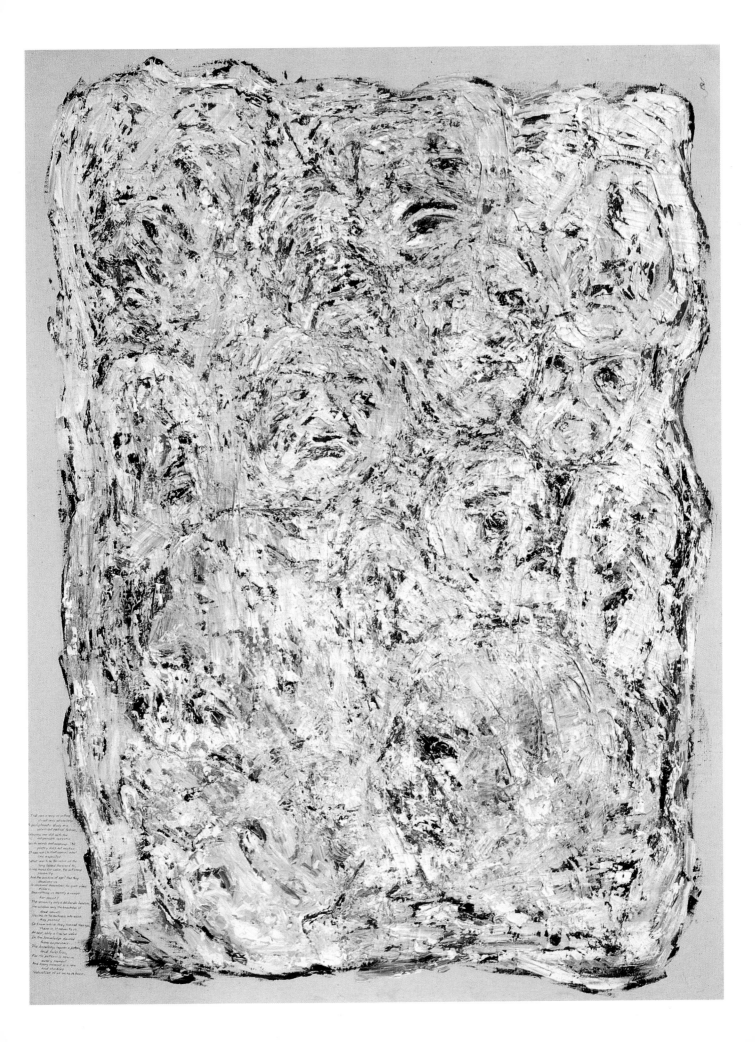

7

We are only undeceived
Of that which deceiving could no longer harm.

9

I said to my soul, be still, and let the dark
come upon you . . .

10

. . . to remind of our and Adam's curse . . .

11

So here I am in the middle way . . .

V

the middle way. ha

largely wasted, the
largely wasted,

to use words, and
words,

start, and a differ
and a

only learned to be

12

. . . old stones that cannot be deciphered.

13

Old men ought to be explorers . . .

14

Where is the end of them, the fishermen sailing
Into the wind's tail, where the fog cowers?

15

Now we come to discover that the moments of agony . . .
are likewise permanent.

16

Time the destroyer is time the preserver . . .

17

Midwinter spring is its own season . . .

18

. . . glow more intense than blaze of branch, or brazier . . .

19

. . . blanched for an hour with transitory blossom
Of snow . . .

20

. . . white again, in May, with voluptuary sweetness.

21

. . . a husk of meaning
From which the purpose breaks only when it is fulfilled.

And what you thought
you came for

Is only a shell, a husk of meaning

From which the purpose breaks only
when it is fulfilled

If at all. Either you had no purpose

Or the purpose is beyond the end you
figured

And is altered in fulfilment.

22

This is the death of air.

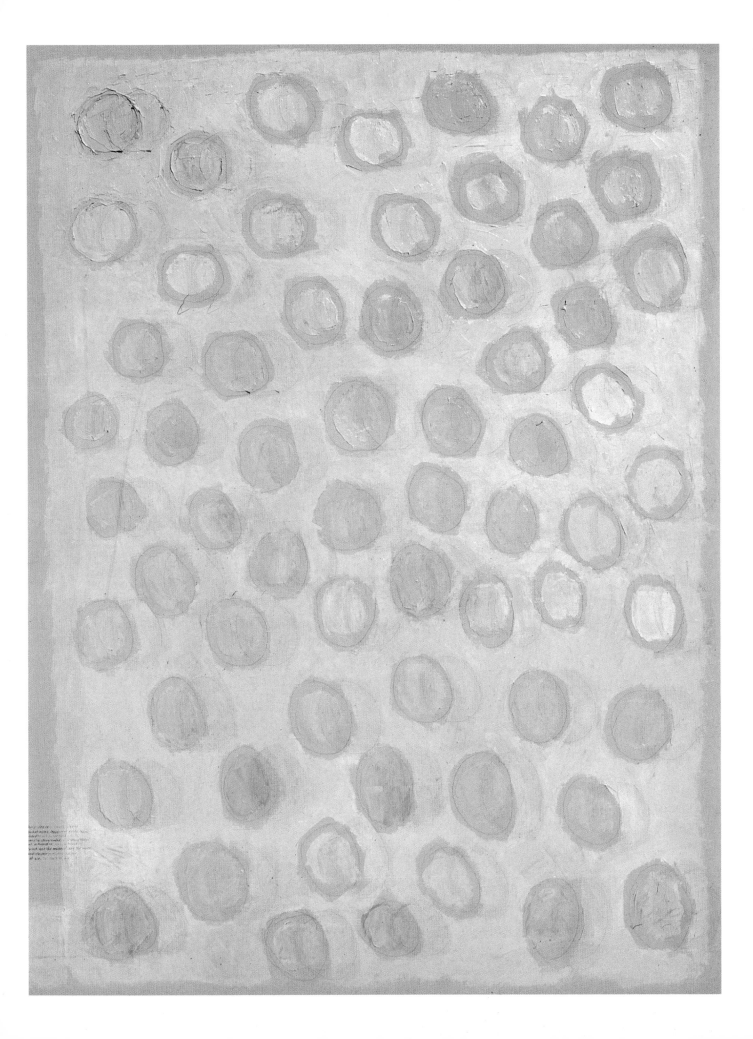

23

This is the death of earth.

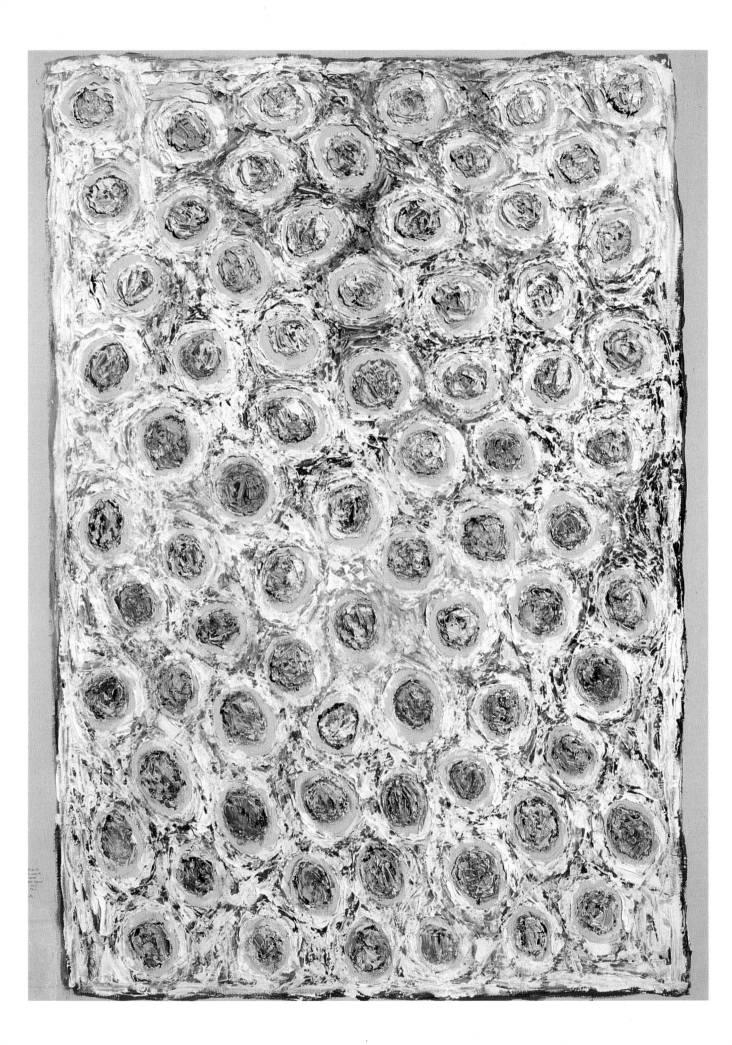

24

This is the death of water and fire.

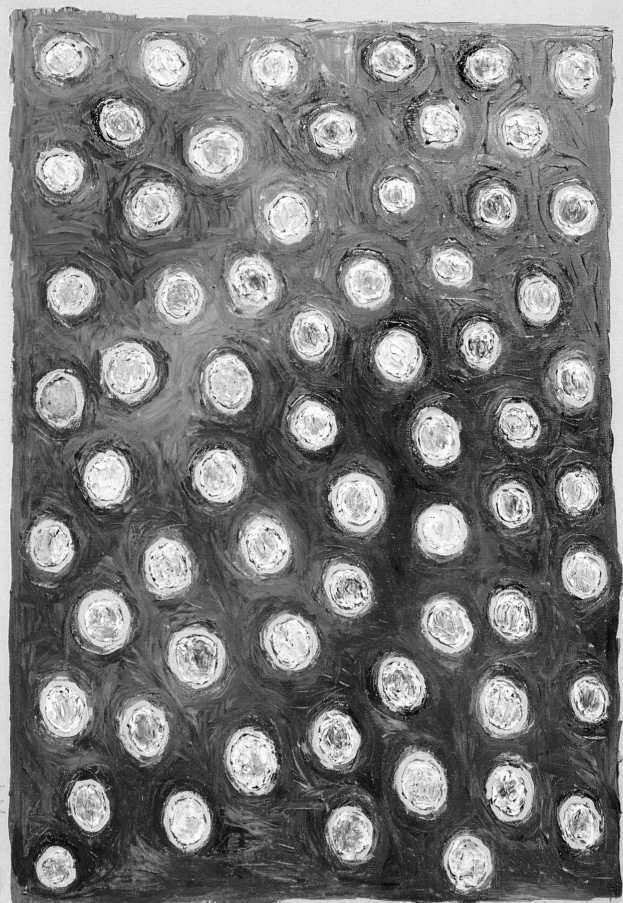

25

I caught the sudden look of some dead master . . .

26

So I assumed a double part . . . .

27

Between two worlds become much like each other . . .

28

. . . the cold friction of expiring sense . . .

29

. . . the conscious impotence of rage
At human folly . . .

30

Of all that you have done, and been . . .

31

There are three conditions which often look alike
Yet differ completely . . .

32

. . . all shall be well, and
All manner of thing shall be well.

33

A symbol perfected in death.

34

The dove descending breaks the air
With flame of incandescent terror . . .

35

We only live, only suspire
Consumed by either fire or fire.

36

Every poem an epitaph.

Every poem an epitaph

37

. . . history is a pattern
Of timeless moments.

38

At the source of the longest river . . .

Afterword

In his essay on Dante (1929), T. S. Eliot stressed the fact that "Dante's is a *visual* imagination." And in the course of a consideration of the nature of allegory, Eliot reflected on the singular process "which led a man having an idea to express it in images." Dante as "competent poet," Eliot held, dealt in "clear visual images." This ability was facilitated by the fact that Dante lived "in an age in which men still saw visions"; contrary to the modern era in which "we take it for granted that our dreams spring from below," the medieval poet pursued the "high vision." Thereby, Dante's poetry—given his "peculiar lucidity" of mind—strives "to make us *see more definitely.*"

While Eliot emphasizes the *visionary* aspect of Dante's art, another process of intellection—one embodying the reverse sequence—can also be seen as operative. As the Aristotle–Aquinas dictum has it: "nothing in the mind that was not first in the senses." It is this principle that James Joyce has his Stephen Dedalus enunciate in *Stephen Hero* (an earlier version of *A Portrait of the Artist as a Young Man*) and ponder in chapter three of *Ulysses*. Through transformation, the visual becomes idea; sense experience becomes intellectual image. Retinal stimuli result in words—abstractions.

As is true with Dante's art, both these processes are evident in Eliot's own *Four Quartets*. While deeply reflecting the structure of music—the late quartets of Beethoven, most evidently—*Four Quartets* is equally rooted in the visual imagination. And as the art of Dante consisted in "making the spiritual visible," so Eliot—dealing as well with the atemporal and the metaphysical—relies upon the "primary pigment of poetry" (as Ezra Pound put it in his "Vortex" manifesto): the image.

In "Burnt Norton," there occurs a moment of spontaneous vision: an empty fountain fills with light.

> . . . To look down into the drained pool.
> Dry the pool, dry concrete, brown edged,
> And the pool was filled with water out of sunlight,
> And the lotos rose, quietly, quietly,
> The surface glittered out of heart of light. . . .

Scattered throughout *Four Quartets* are such intensely *visual* events— instants of suspension in which the temporal pattern is pierced—glimpsed quickly, "sudden in a shaft of sunlight." Visual details are woven into the very fabric of the poem's tapestry: "the dust on a bowl of rose-leaves"; "garlic and sapphire in the mud"; "the rank ailanthus of the April dooryard"; "the hedgerow . . . blanched for an hour with transitory blossom / Of snow. . . ." Intermixed with statements of metaphysical abstraction, vibrant images of visual perception play in intellectual counterpoint.

Evident as well is the process of *transformation*, of the sensate become intellectual. Such a statement as "Dust inbreathed was a house" reflects this primary process. The stone walls of a house demolished during a raid in the London *Blitz* have become "dust in the air suspended"—capable of being directly experienced by the senses; yet the extreme condensation of statement renders the experience abstract. Likewise, the strafing Luftwaffe plane is metamorphosed: "The dove descending breaks the air / With flame of incandescent terror. . . ." In the poem, the sensate is transmuted into abstraction—by means of such intense, compressed images.

What visual experiences might Eliot have encountered on that clear spring day in May 1936 when—after having turned "behind the pig-sty"— he first visited Nicholas Ferrar's chapel at Little Gidding? Did such visual germs become stored in the deep recesses of Eliot's mind (as fragments shored against ruin) to sprout later into words? Is this not the very essence of the metamorphosis enacted by contemplation?

Parallel to this process is that which germinated in David Finn's paintings. These are not only "obsessions" (as Stephen Spender has dubbed them) but also "meditations." The sense experience—of words seen clearly on the page; of words which left images on the retina of the intellect; of words heard in the inner mind—creates new visual blooms, evoking the original sources. By the painter's allowing Eliot's spermatic words to echo in his memory, these paintings have come to fruition: new shoots from buried roots.

John Walsh